hamlyn

flowers, leaves and seeds

Photography by Linda Burgess

Janet Grant

Contents

First published in Great Britain in 1999
by Hamlyn, an imprint of Octopus Publishing Group Limited,
2–4 Heron Quays, London E14 4JP

A CIP catalogue record of this book is available from the British Library

ISBN 0 600 59474 2

Printed and bound in China

Publishing Director: Laura Bamford

Creative Director: Keith Martin
Design: Mark Winwood, Ruth Hope

Executive Editor: Polly Manguel
Project Editor: Joanna Smith
Assistant Editor: Cara Frost

Production Controller: Katherine Hockley

Introduction

The art of creating designs from all kinds of natural materials has progressed considerably from the days, not so long ago, when a white basket full of helichrysum and statis was considered to be the last word in floral design. However, what has gone before very often looks jaded and shabby when compared to current fashions, and I have no doubt that many of the designs in this book will look rather tired if recreated in 20 years.

The exciting thing about natural design ideas at the moment is the variety of ingredients which are now available, from freeze-dried roses to handmade java flowers from India. With the advance in commercial drying techniques and new preservation methods, there has never been such a wide choice of foliage and flowers. Seed pods and shells are available from locations around the world and provide an incredible source of shapes and textures when creating arrangements. Combine these with the profusion of wonderful containers, and it is possible for anyone to create beautiful pieces for their homes.

Once you have mastered the basics of natural design and have become more confident, you will have endless scope for creating ideas which can be developed into your own finished work. I often find that the simplest ideas work the best. For example, what could look more stunning than a beautiful glass vase filled with dried giant cardoons which can be grown in your garden?

Many designs today are kept very simple and have a more sculptured appearance than the delicate and more complicated arrangements of the past. A wider selection of colourful ingredients are available too, from pastel stone-washed shades to vibrant primary colours. Many products today, follow the latest fashion trends and colours, and dried flowers are no exception. So there is no excuse, keep on reading and start designing!

Janet Grant

10–15 minutes

This milky white heart, finished with a sprig of pretty cottage garden flowers and herbs, will add a romantic touch wherever you hang it.

Rice hearts

What you need...

- Scrap paper
- Pen
- Polystyrene square
- Craft knife
- Shallow dish
- Border paste
- Small paint brush
- Skewer
- Cotton string
- Medium gauge florist's wire
- Glue gun
- Scissors

Natural materials
- White rice
- Dried white larkspur
- Preserved or dried rosemary

...and some tips!

- *Cut the 'V' at the top of the heart slightly deeper than you think necessary as it fills up considerably when the rice is glued on.*

- *Why not give these pretty rice hearts to wedding guests as an unusual gift, rather than the traditional sugared almonds? Just add a small, simple tag giving the names of the bride and groom and the date of the wedding.*

Basic shape

1 Draw your heart on to scrap paper and cut around it to make a template. Trace around the template on to the polystyrene, then cut out the heart with a craft knife. Pour the rice into a shallow dish. Brush border paste onto one edge of the heart and press firmly into the rice. Repeat this until the whole heart is covered. Gently press any stray rice grains into place. Using a skewer, make a hole approximately 1 cm (½ inch) deep in the central 'V', ready for your hanging loop. Allow the heart to dry.

Hanging it up

2 Cut a length of cotton string to make a hanging loop. Fold it in half and bind the two loose ends together with florist's wire. Twist the ends of the wire together and cut them off to leave a rigid wire stump. Push the wire end into the hole you made with the skewer and fix it in place using a glue gun.
Make sure that the wire is hidden inside the hole and only the string is visible.

Romantic touch

3 Select and cut a pretty larkspur tip and rosemary sprig, then bind them together with string to form a dainty bouquet. Take the bouquet and position it on the heart. When you've decided where it looks best, glue it in place permanently to finish.
Make sure the little bouquet is in keeping with the size of the heart: the top and bottom tips should just touch the edges of the heart.

Harvest harmony

What you need...

- Knife
- Dry oasis foam
- Ivory coloured long tom pot
- Glue gun

Natural materials
- Bleached oats
- Round dried chillies
- Moss

...and some tips!

- *To ensure that the arrangement is even, continually turn the pot as you are putting in each bunch of oats. Also check the height and straightness of each bunch as you build up the desired shape.*

- *This arrangement is good for a bright windowsill as the oats have already been bleached and will not fade much more. However, the chillies and moss will fade, so turn the arrangement occasionally so it will fade evenly.*

Sun-bleached oats and glossy red chillies offer a reminder of long, late summer days, whatever the season.

Equal lengths

1 Use the knife to cut the foam down to fit inside the pot. The foam does not have to be in one piece, as long as the pot is tightly filled with foam. Divide the oats into small bundles of about 20 stems, and arrange the heads so that they are all level. Trim the stems of each bunch to the same length. *This is a tall, elegant arrangement so the oats should be taller than the height of the pot. At this stage you may want to wire each bunch if you feel the stems are too brittle to push straight into the foam.*

Filling the pot

2 Starting in the centre of the pot, push one bunch of oats at a time into the oasis. Make sure you hold the bunch firmly at its base, keeping it as upright as possible as you push it into the foam. Gradually build up a dense block of oats, making sure that the tips are all level.

Remember you have to leave room for the chillies, so don't arrange the oats too close to the edge of the pot.

Selecting the best

3 Look through the chillies and pick out the best ones, selecting those of a similar size and shape. Arrange the chillies around the outside of the oats with the tips of the chillies hanging over the edge of the pot. Place a generous blob of glue onto the back of each chilli and press firmly in place on to the oasis. When the chillies are firmly glued in place in a ring around the oats, there will still be small areas of oasis showing through. These bald spots can easily be hidden by pushing small pieces of woodland moss into the gaps between the chillies. *If you let go of the chilli before the glue has dried, the chilli will not stick. Be patient!*

Bold bundles

What you need...

- Scissors
- Medium gauge florist's wire

Natural materials
- Dried grass stems
- Coloured raffia

...and some tips!

- *When making other arrangements using dried grasses, keep the discarded stems which will build up your stock for this project.*

Bold and strong, these regimented bundles of grass stems are perfect for contemporary room settings. Display them alone, or in groups of three for greater impact.

Bundling up

1 Take a small handful of grass and cut it to the required finished length. Repeat, cutting each handful to the same length. Gather the grasses together to form a large bundle, gently tapping any stray grasses into place so that the ends are even. Secure the bundle by loosely tying a piece of wire around the centre. Grasp the bundle around the middle with both hands and tap the end down firmly on a work surface. This will give a perfect flat base. Tighten the wire around the grasses to prevent them moving, then trim the tops if necessary to make them all equal lengths.

Tying the knot

2 Take a handful of raffia in your chosen colour and arrange the strands so they form a neat bunch. Finish the bundle by tying the raffia tightly around the centre, covering the wire. Tie the raffia in a knot, pulling it quite tight. A neat, double knot will hold the raffia in position. When you are happy with the look of the knot, trim the ends of the raffia neatly and evenly to the same length.

Repeat the process with more bundles, if required, making them the same or different sizes and varying the colour of the raffia.

A touch of luxury at Christmas, with golden holly leaves and bright shining beads. Finish the wreath with a delicate tulle ribbon for an opulent effect.

All that glitters

What you need...

- Gold spray paint
- Secateurs
- Medium gauge florist's wire
- Gold florist's wire
- Pearl beads on wire stems
- Gold tulle ribbon bow

Natural materials
- Dried holly oak branches
- Bark-covered wreath base

...and some tips!

- *Take care when separating the sprigs of leaves from the branches as holly can be quite brittle.*

- *It is important when using spray paint, to adequately cover work surfaces and surrounding areas. Also make sure that you have plenty of ventilation and avoid breathing in the fumes. If possible, it is better to do all spraying outside.*

1

Adding the bow

3 When the wreath is complete, and you are happy with the overall arrangement of leaves and beads, complete the wreath by attaching the gold tulle bow, pulling the gold wire tightly over the centre of the bow several times to fix it in place. Cut the gold wire and wrap it around the wreath to secure it.

Make sure the end of the wire is securely finished off as disaster will strike if it becomes loose. (A small drip of glue will help).

Midas touch

1 Start by spraying the holly branches gold, turning them as you spray to ensure an even colour. When dry, trim the holly into shorter lengths, taking care to cut the stems neatly at a joint so that the cut ends are less visible in the finished wreath. Next attach a wire hanging loop to the back of the bark-covered wreath base.

Round in circles

2 Take the reel of gold wire and secure it to the wreath by winding it around several times. Divide the holly and pearls into four piles and work on one quarter of the wreath at a time to achieve an even spread of materials.

Lay the first sprig of holly on to the wreath, then pull the wire over the stem and around the wreath. Continue to add sprigs, all facing the same direction, with the leaves of each sprig overlapping the stems of the last. Add a small bunch of pearls at regular intervals, continuously checking the shape.

It is important to keep the wire tight. If necessary, bind it around each stem twice to keep the ingredients firmly secured.

Evoke memories of days at the seaside by using your collection of shells to create a simple, decorated pot to hold a pure white church candle.

Down by the sea

What you need...

- Spray glue
- Glue gun
- Medium bowl
- Scissors
- Dry oasis foam
- Candle
- Knife

Natural materials
- Terracotta pot
- Dry fine sand
- Natural twine
- Grey moss or lichen
- Shells

...and some tips!

- *When cutting out the foam to make a hole for the candle to fit snugly, cut just inside the line you have marked. Remember that you can always remove some more of the foam if the hole is not large enough.*

- *This display can be used to brighten up almost any room. The seaside theme makes it good for a bathroom, but why not try it as a table centrepiece for a relaxed meal?*

Sandy coating

1 Check that the pot is clean and dry. Holding it by the rim, spray the bottom two thirds with glue. Quickly sprinkle sand evenly over the glued area, turning the pot as you do so. Place the empty bowl underneath to catch the excess sand. When dry, tap the pot gently to remove excess sand which has not stuck. If you require a sandier finish simply repeat the process. Wind twine around the pot just under the rim and secure with a simple knot. A small blob of hot glue under the knot will make sure that it remains in place.

Foam filling

2 Fill the pot with foam, then place the candle on top in the middle and mark around its circumference with a knife. Remove the candle and cut out the circle you have marked to approximately 4 cm (1½ inches) deep. Place the candle into the hole, pressing down firmly, until it feels secure.

Adding moss and shells

3 Tease out the moss or lichen and using the glue gun, glue it around the base of the candle to cover the oasis sparingly. Then stick three of the largest shells in place, spacing them evenly around the candle. Fill each section in turn, gluing the larger shells in place first and filling in any gaps with smaller ones.

Try not to get too carried away with the number of shells you use or you may lose the interesting outlines and end up with an arrangement which is too cluttered.

Shades of blue

What you need...

- Small plastic bag
- Gift bag and tag
- Dry oasis foam
- Scissors

Natural materials
- Dry sand
- Dried dark blue larkspur
- Dried light blue larkspur
- Woodland moss

...and some tips!

- *For an even more personal gift, decorate the gift bag yourself using spray paints or acrylic paints. Choose a design, it can be as simple or as complicated as you like.*

- *If the gift bag is quite small, cut the foam block to size with a knife.*

A vibrant arrangement of light and dark blue larkspur and woodland moss, ready to go in its own matching gift bag – the perfect present for an artistic friend.

Weighing down

1 Half fill the small plastic bag with sand and secure with a knot. Drop this into the bottom of the gift bag where it will act as a simple but effective weight, preventing the finished arrangement from toppling over. Next place the oasis block in the gift bag on top of the sand weight.

Adding the flowers

2 Separate the stems of larkspur and trim each down to about the same length, remembering that they will be pushed into the foam. Test one first to check the length before cutting all of them. Starting in the centre, fill the oasis with larkspur stems with as few gaps as possible. Make the centre stems slightly taller and gradually lean the stems outwards as you reach the front and sides of the arrangement. Keep the stems at the back upright so that they do not get broken when the arrangement is placed against a wall. *As this is an informal arrangement, the larkspur heads should be at different heights. Remember to mix the light and dark colours as you go.*

Mossy cover up

3 Fill in any remaining gaps around the base of the stems, by gently pressing small amounts of moss between the stems so that the finished arrangement has no oasis showing.

1

Decorative soaps

What you need...

- White soaps with straight sides
- White parcel string
- Scissors
- Glue gun
- Artificial white chrysanthemums

Natural materials
- Preserved dark green magnolia leaves

...and some tips!

- *If it makes it easier, hold the leaves in place using a few dress-making pins while you are tying the string in position.*

- *Preserved leaves often leave dye on your hands, so be careful not to touch the soap where green fingerprints might be visible.*

Pure white bars of soap are elegantly wrapped in dark, glossy leaves. Arrange several wrapped soaps in a white bowl or dish – the finishing touch to a beautiful bathroom.

Cover up

1 Sort your leaves into pairs of roughly equal size and shape. Each leaf should be large enough to cover at least two-thirds of the soap when wrapped around it. Wrap the first leaf around the soap, covering one flat side. Place the largely uncovered side down on top of the second leaf and wrap it tightly around to cover the soap. Wrap the string around the leaves twice, pulling tightly. Lay the soap down on a work surface and secure the string with a simple knot.

Finishing touch

2 Cut off any surplus string to leave two short ends, using the scissors. Finish off by placing some hot glue on the back of a chrysanthemum head and push the flower gently in place on top of the knot.

Hold it still until the glue dries or the flower will not stay put.

A wonderful combination of intense colours and exciting textures creates a stunning centrepiece.

Dome of java

What you need...

- Dry oasis foam
- Fine garden canes
- Glue gun
- Knife
- Scissors
- Wire cutters

Natural materials
- Black cardboard box
- Grey telanchila moss
- Pintado hearts
- Palm fruits (Plums)
- Java flowers (Burgundy)
- Strawberry corns (round)
- Strawberry corns (long)

...and some tips!

- *Choose a box which is approximately 12 cm (5 inches) square to begin with, as this arrangement uses a lot of ingredients.*

Adding oasis

1 Fill the box with oasis, adding a second block on top of the first. This second block should be approximately two-thirds of the size of the base. Hold in place using short pieces of garden cane pushed into the base with their tops protruding. Gently push the second block down onto the cane tips which you have left, this will hold the oasis in place. Glue telanchila moss on to the oasis allowing it to hang over the edge of the box.

Gluing and trimming

2 Trim down the stems of the flowers and seed heads to approximately 15 cm (6 inches). Start to build your outline shape by placing one pintado heart in the centre of the top oasis, then one at each corner where the two oasis blocks meet.

Plums and stems

3 As the plums are the largest ingredient to be used and are very sturdy, add them all at this stage, continually turning the arrangement to check that they are being distributed evenly. Allow some of them to hang over the edge of the box giving the effect of a softer outline. To do this, push the stems at an upward angle into the top foam block.

Building up

4 Now build up your display to create a well-filled dome. Keep some of the long corns until the end, as they will be useful for filling any remaining small gaps. The aim is for the arrangement to have an even mix of shapes and textures as this will be a centre-piece and it will be seen from all sides.

4

Picture perfect

What you need...

- Sandpaper
- Square picture frame
- Scissors
- Glue gun

Natural materials
- Dried yellow roses
- Small preserved leaves

...and some tips!

- *If the rose heads are squashed or mis-shapen, steam them to open them up a little (see page 132).*

- *To preserve the colour and texture of the roses, you can spray them with a coat of florist's clear sealant. Remember, though, that if you have steamed the rose heads, leave them to cool down and dry off properly before spraying, otherwise you may be trapping moisture inside which could cause them to rot.*

Yellow country garden roses decorate this simple square picture frame to create an elegant border for your photographs.

Stem support

1 Gently use the sandpaper to create a key on the surface of the frame where the roses will be attached. This will help the glue to stick to the frame. Cut off the rose heads and set aside. Remove the leaves from the straightest stems and trim the stems down to equal lengths, slightly longer than the width of the opening in the picture frame. Glue the stems in position on either side of the frame, leaving a gap between each pair. These gaps will act as a channel into which the rose heads will be glued. Finish off the ends by gluing some small preserved leaves to the frame.

Adding the flowers

2 Carefully place the rose heads into the channels separating the stems. Take care not to position them too close together or you may crush the petals. Finally, glue them in position to complete the frame.

You may need to hold each flower head in place until the glue dries to make sure they are firmly attached.

Simply stunning

What you need...

- Square terracotta vase
- Dry oasis foam
- Knife
- Medium gauge florist's wire
- Wire cutters
- Secateurs

Natural materials
- Dyed preserved lotus leaves
- Contorted willow stems
- Dyed dried allium heads

...and some tips!

- *Do not arrange the willow stems too close together as you will not have enough space for the thick allium stems.*

- *It is easier to use secateurs to cut the thicker stems.*

Sculptural contorted willow makes the perfect foil for the bold shapes of giant allium heads and lotus leaves arranged in a terracotta vase.

1

2

Wired up

1 Fill the vase with foam, cutting the blocks with a knife as necessary to ensure a close fit. Select about eight lotus leaves of a similar size, then wire them individually (see page 132) to give them long, firm wire stems.

Matt side up

2 The leaves have a glossy side and a matt side. Push the wired stems into the foam with the matt sides of the leaves facing upwards.

The leaves should be arranged to form a loose collar around the top of the vase. Try not to make the arrangement too regimented.

Adding structure

3 Trim the ends of the contorted willow stems at an angle to form a point. This will make it much easier to push them into the foam. Using the thickest and tallest branches first, push them into the foam between the lotus leaves to create an informal fan of twigs. Cut the allium stems down to the right length, again giving them a pointed end. Hold the stems firm at the top and bottom as you insert them into the foam, to prevent them breaking.

As the willow stems are contorted, you may find that you keep coming across willow stems as you try to insert the alliums. There is no set pattern for arranging the allium stems, as long as the finished display looks balanced.

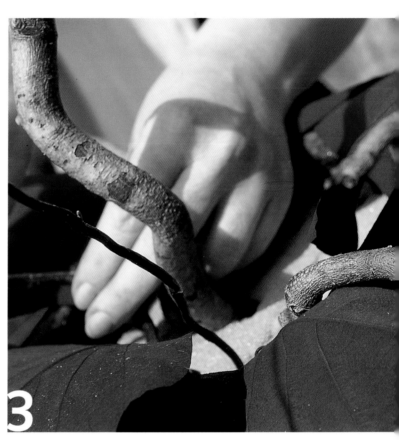

3

Delicate chrysanthemums nestle in a cloud of creamy white gypsophila.

Tall basket

What you need...

- Dry oasis foam
- Newspaper
- Knife
- Scissors

Natural Materials
- Tall rustic basket
- Woodland moss
- Gypsophila
- Spider chrysanthemums
- Salignum

...and some tips!

- *Dry your own gypsophila as it often looks better than shop bought. Just hang it upside down until dry, remembering to detangle it while it is still fresh.*

Blocking the basket

1 As this basket is tall and narrow, it is not necessary to fill the whole of it with oasis. Pack the bottom third with scrunched up newspaper making sure it is firm. Add a solid block of oasis, pushing it firmly into place. Most of the flowers used in this arrangement are very fine and light so it is unnecessary to completely fill the top of the basket. Fill gaps at the sides of the oasis block with moss before you begin the arrangement. Before using the gypsophila, gently tease the stems apart so that they are all separated. Be especially careful as the flowers are often quite tangled and are quite prone to breaking.

Gently does it

2 You are going to create a soft cloud effect of gypsophila as your basic shape. Start by trimming down the stems, if necessary splitting them into small sprigs. Always cut the stems at a joint to give a neater finish as well as less wastage. Carefully push the gypsophila stems vertically into the oasis starting in the centre, and gradually insert them at an angle as you work your way outwards. Turn the basket as you do this, checking the shape of the arrangement as you go.

Clouds of flowers

3 Trim the stems of the spider chysanthemums and salignum. Starting in the centre, add the salignum, gently holding the gypsophila to one side, to prevent it breaking. Add the spider chrysanthemums in the same way, spacing them evenly between the salignum, and pushing the flower heads in, so that they lie just below the level of the gypsophila.

Fruitful frame

What you need...

- Bowl
- Deep box frame
- Spray glue
- Glue gun

Natural materials
- Yellow lentils
- Green mung beans
- Dried whole oranges
- Orange java flower heads

...and some tips!

- *Rather than buy dried oranges, why not make you own? (See page 134)*

Citrus fruits, mixed pulses and exotic flower heads create a tapestry of colour in the perfect kitchen picture.

Making the base

1 Mix the lentils and beans in a bowl. Spray the back of the box frame with glue and wait until it is tacky. Gently sprinkle the pulses over the glued area until completely covered and press them down gently to ensure they connect with the glued surface. Leave to dry, then turn the box upside down so that any loose pulses will fall off.

If any bare patches remain, repeat the gluing process until adequate coverage is achieved.

Adding the features

2 Select some oranges and flower heads of a similar size. Place them in a pattern on top of the pulses, then glue in place using the glue gun. Leave the glue to dry before hanging the frame.

The oranges are fairly heavy so be generous with the glue to ensure they stay in place once the frame is hung.

Clear perfection

What you need...

- Small glass containers
- Florist's plasticine
- Scissors
- Dry oasis foam
- Knife

Natural materials.
- Small twigs
- Moss
- Lavender grains
- Dried red roses
- Dried lavender
- Dried rice grass

...and some tips!

- *A large variety of ingredients can be used to conceal the foam. Try sand, lentils or brightly-coloured bath crystals as an alternative.*

- *Group the vases together on a dressing table to fill the room with the heady scent of lavender.*

A collection of simple glass vases full of your favourite flowers, such as sweet scented lavender and cottage garden roses, echoes pretty bedroom chintzes.

Offering support

1 Glass containers cannot be filled with oasis in the normal way due to their transparency. First place a mound of plasticine in the centre of the vase, making sure it is firmly attached to the base. Trim a small twig to three-quarters of the height of the vase. Push the twig down into the centre of the plasticine, leaving a vertical spike.

Repeat with the other vases: they are all treated in exactly the same way.

A good fit

2 Cut a piece of oasis into a cylinder which is smaller than each of the containers. Press the oasis firmly on to the twig spike. Check to ensure that there is a gap between the oasis and the glass sides. Fill in the gap between the foam and the vase with moss or lavender grains, making sure that the foam is not visible. Trim the stems of the roses, lavender and grass to the required length. If necessary, steam the rose heads (see page 132). Arrange each of the flower types in a different glass vase. Build up your blocks of colour, starting in the centre of the oasis, pushing the stems in closely together and working towards the outer rim.

Remember to check the shape of your arrangement frequently, turning it as you add more ingredients. Cover any remaining oasis around the rim with more moss or lavender grains.

Scented elegance

Softly frosted grey-green eucalyptus, with its wonderful musky fragrance, creates a strong and simple yet elegant winter display.

What you need...

- Pin holder
- Glass vase
- Florist's plasticine
- Dry oasis foam
- Knife
- Scissors

Natural materials
- Rock salt
- Grey-green preserved eucalyptus

...and some tips!

- *This arrangement is wonderfully effective when displayed in front of a window, giving a strong silhouette of eucalyptus and glass.*

- *Rock salt is a lovely pure white, but you could add a splash of colour to this display by using coloured bath crystals instead.*

A firm base

1 Fix the pin holder to the base of the vase using a piece of florist's plasticine. Cut the block of oasis to roughly the same shape as the bottom of the vase; you need it to be about half as high as the vase and approximately 1 cm (½ inch) less in diameter than the vase. Push the oasis block firmly on to the pin holder, making sure that it is kept straight and does not touch the sides of the vase. Check again that it is held securely in place and does not shake.

A pinch of salt

2 Gradually fill the gap around the oasis with rock salt. Pour it carefully until it is level with, but not covering, the top of the oasis.

Gently rocking the vase from side to side will ensure that there are no gaps in the salt.

A fan of foliage

3 Separate the eucalyptus branches and trim them to the desired length, using scissors. Strip the leaves from the portion of stem which is going to be pushed into the oasis, but no higher. Holding each branch at its base, push it firmly down into the foam. Keep them as straight as possible in the centre and then gently fan them outwards as you reach the sides. To cover the top of the oasis, gently pull the eucalyptus back and pour in more salt.

Rock the vase lightly from side to side to level the salt and remove any crystals lodged amongst the leaves. Although the eucalyptus gives a strong outline, it is softened by allowing the branches to fan outwards over the hard edge of the vase.

1

Marigolds in wax

What you need...

- Absorbent kitchen paper
- White utility candles
- Old saucepan
- Wax thermometer (optional)
- Scissors
- Lime green pillar candle
- Square metal plate

Natural materials
- Fresh marigolds
- Dried kumquats (see page 134)
- Dried clementines (see page 134)

...and some tips!

- *Many other fresh flowers are suitable for waxing. Experiment with roses, hyacinths and stephanotis.*

- *Waxed flowers make ideal cake decorations, but make sure nobody tries to eat them.*

Vibrant orange marigolds, kumquats and clementines nestle around a refreshing lime green candle, a perfect display for summer entertaining. This is a temporary display, lasting a week at most, but it is well worth the effort.

Taking the plunge

1 Make sure that the marigolds are completely dry, pat them gently with kitchen paper if necessary. Melt the utility candles gently in the saucepan. A wax thermometer is useful as wax which is too hot will scorch the flowers, while wax which is too cold will not cover the flowers effectively, 65.5°C (150°F) is ideal. Cut the flower stems down, discarding any leaves. Hold the flower stem and dip the head completely into the hot wax.

Arranging the petals

2 Lift the flower out immediately, allowing excess wax to drip back into the saucepan. As the wax will take around 30 seconds to harden, you have time to gently rearrange the petals if necessary. But be careful not to touch the hot wax too soon! Repeat this with each of the flower stems. Place the pillar candle in the centre of the plate and arrange the kumquats and clementines around its base. Finally trim down the marigold stems, if necessary, and arrange the flowers amongst the fruits, inserting the stems in the gaps.

15–20 minutes

Sumptuous peach roses and pink larkspur, arranged in a box gently wrapped in soft sea-blue tissue paper.

Box of blooms

What you need...

- Small square cardboard box
- Dry oasis foam
- Knife
- 2 sheets of blue tissue paper
- Elastic band
- Parcel string
- Scissors

Natural materials
- Freeze-dried peach roses
- Dried pink larkspur
- Dried salal leaves
- Woodland moss

...and some tips!

- *Handle the roses very carefully, supporting the stems as you insert them into the foam and remember that their weakest point is where the stem joins the head.*

- *If any of the rose heads look squashed, they can be gently steamed (see page 132) to help them regain a good shape. But be very careful when doing this to avoid damaging them.*

Box clever

1 Fill the cardboard box with foam, cutting it to size with a knife (see page 134). Lay a sheet of tissue flat on the work surface. Place the box in the centre and fold the tissue up and around it on all sides. Repeat with the other sheet of tissue and secure the paper in place with an elastic band. Wind parcel string around the box several times, covering the elastic band and securing with a simple knot. *Make sure that the corners of the tissue are evenly spaced around the top of the box as this will make the arrangement look balanced when finished. Tease out and arrange the corners as necessary.*

Arranging the flowers

2 Trim the flower stems to equal lengths and strip off the leaves. Cut the branches of salal leaves into smaller pieces, cutting at a leaf joint to avoid wastage and create a better finish. Reserving the nicest roses for the front of the arrangement, insert the first rose stem in the centre of the oasis. Check its height is roughly the same as that of the box. Add the larkspur and salal leaves around the rose, leaving them slightly taller to act as a shield. Build up the arrangement, frequently checking the overall shape along with the mix of flowers and leaves. As you get towards the edge of the box, push the stems in at a slight angle to give a soft dome shape when finished. Cover any visible oasis around the edge with woodland moss.

These decorative mossy cubes, perfumed with essential oils, make a refreshing change to pot pourri.

Scented cubes

What you need...

- Ruler
- Dry oasis foam
- Knife
- Glue gun
- Green fine gauge florist's wire

Natural materials
- Woodland moss
- Silica-dried zinnia flowers
- Essential oils

...and some tips!

- *You can dry your own flowers in silica (see page 135). Dahlias, roses, peonies and rudbeckias are some of the easiest flowers to preserve in this way.*

- *As an alternative decoration, you can stick pieces of dried bark among the moss pieces, to add more texture. Dried leaves could be used instead of moss. Stick them on to the surface of the cube in the same way.*

Measuring up

1 Measure the foam and cut it to form a cube. Sort through the moss and pick out the largest pieces. Cover one side of the cube in hot glue and lay pieces of moss on top, fitting the pieces together like a patchwork. Press down firmly until the glue sets. Repeat with the other sides.

You may need quite a lot of glue as the underside of the moss can be rather earthy, so it pays to give it a shake prior to gluing!

A neat appearance

2 When your cube is completely covered in moss, fix the florist's wire to the cube by pushing the end well into the foam and, if necessary using a small drop of hot glue. Holding the cube in one hand, begin to wind the wire around it, pulling it just tight enough so that the wire does not slice through the moss and oasis. Cut the wire when you are happy with the shape and push the end into the foam, as before.

Wind the wire quite randomly, turning the cube so that all sides are covered. It helps to pull the moss flat and gives a more defined cube shape.

Adding fragrance

3 To complete the decoration of your cube, glue a single zinnia flower on one side. Finally, add a few drops of essential oil to perfume the cube.

Only apply the oil to the top of the cube as it may damage polished surfaces.

Bean balls

What you need...

- Newspaper
- Brush
- Polystyrene balls
- Border adhesive
- Bowl of water
- Red and black acrylic paints
- Acrylic glue
- Clear varnish (optional)

Natural materials
- Red beans
- Black beans

...and some tips!

- *Any type of bean can be used to make these balls. There are many available in different colours and patterns, so experiment to see what attractive effects you can create.*

- *For a variation, use alternate rows of black and red beans, or create other patterns using two different colours.*

Bright, shiny bean balls look great and make an unusual and longer lasting variation on bowls of fruit.

A good base

1 Tear the newspaper into strips, 2 cm (¾ inch) wide and about 15 cm (6 inches) long. Brush half of the surface of the ball with border adhesive. Dip the strips of newspaper in the bowl of water, one at a time, shake off the excess water, then stick them to the glued surface of the ball. Continue until the glued half of the ball is covered, then repeat the process with the other half of the ball. Leave to dry.

Ready to glue

2 Paint the balls with the acrylic paints and allow to dry. Apply two coats if necessary. Next, spread acrylic glue over half the surface of the ball. Starting in the centre, stick the largest beans on to the surface of the ball. Arrange them so that they are all facing in the same direction in a ring around the centre of the ball.

Spilling the beans

3 Continue to add rows of beans on the glued surface, using increasingly smaller beans as you move towards the top of the ball. Spread glue on the second half and stick the beans in place as before, then leave to dry. *If necessary, change the direction of the beans to give a neat finish and ensure they fit. To make the finished ball more durable, cover with a coat of clear varnish, if desired.*

Moss topiary

What you need...

- Secateurs
- 2 dry oasis foam balls
- Glue gun
- Mossing pins
- Dry oasis foam block
- Knife
- White trellis planter

Natural materials
- 2 straight sticks
- Green reindeer moss
- Pea gravel
- 2 small terracotta pots
- 2 medium terracotta pots

...and some tips!

- *When covering the oasis spheres with moss, handle the trunks as little as possible to prevent them loosening.*

- *This formal display is ideal for a mantlepiece or shelf in a cosy sitting room. Alternatively, use it to decorate a conservatory or garden room.*

Recreate the essence of the English formal garden with stylish topiary trees in an immaculate white trellis planter. Just as effective and easier to make than the real thing.

Starting out

1 Cut one end of each stick to form a point. Push the pointed tip of the stick gently into the oasis ball by about 2 cm (1 inch) and remove. Fill the hole with hot glue and then push the stick back into the sphere, checking to ensure that it is being pushed towards the centre of the oasis. Repeat with the other stick and ball.

Covering with moss

2 Cut any large pieces of moss into smaller shapes. Start to cover the foam balls with moss, one piece at a time, slightly overlapping each one, so that there are no gaps. Hold the moss in place with mossing pins.

Try not to use too many pins as they will tend to show and detract from the wonderful texture of the moss.

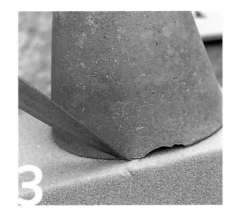

Trimming the foam

3 Place a small pot, rim side down, on the foam block and mark around it with a knife. Take the pot away and trim the foam to fit snugly in the pot, following your marks and turning frequently. Don't cut away too much foam at once. You can always cut more away if the foam is too big, but you can't easily put some back.

Securing the base

4 Push the foam firmly into the pot and repeat with the other small pot, leaving room for the gravel on top. The foam should be wedged firmly in place without any room for movement. Insert the base of each tree trunk in the middle of the foam in one of the small pots. Gently push straight down until the tree is standing firm.

Filling the pots

5 Cover the top of the oasis with pea gravel. Fill the bottom of the larger pots with more gravel then stand the finished trees on top and check the levels. The rim of the smaller pot should sit above the level of the larger pot. Now drop more gravel into the larger pots and fill them to the rim. Place the two trees in their gravel-filled pots side by side in the trellis planter. If the planter is very long, use three or more trees in a row.

More than a hint of the Scottish Highlands here, in a textural display of spiky cardoons, silver blue globe thistles, sea holly and a touch of bonnie heather.

Highland fling

What you need...

- Galvanised metal urn
- Dry oasis foam
- Knife
- Scissors
- Medium gauge florist's wire

Natural materials
- Dried globe thistle (*Echinops*)
- Dried cardoons
- Preserved heather
- Dried sea holly (*Eryngium*)

...and some tips!

- *Fill in any gaps with a few more sprigs of heather if you need to, so that the arrangement has a uniform shape.*

Creating shape

1 Start by filling the urn with foam, cutting it to size with a knife (see page 134). You may need more than one piece if it is a large urn. Simply wedge the pieces in together to fit snugly inside the urn. Separate out the flowers, trimming down the stems if necessary. Start the arrangement by using the globe thistles to create the initial shape. Aim for a soft dome, with the flowers around the sides gently breaking up the rim of the urn.

Filling in

2 Gradually add the cardoons between the globe thistle stems, rotating the urn frequently to check your arrangement for uniform texture and colour. Make sure the flowers are of slightly varying heights to add interest and depth to the display. Wire the heather sprigs into small bundles to give them more impact (see page 132). Add the heather bundles between the other flowers, then the sea holly, which is prickly so should be left until last.

A fascinating mix of intriguing exotics provides colour and texture in a terracotta drainpipe.

Exotic touch

What you need...

- Terracotta drain-pipe
- Corrugated cardboard
- Pen
- Glue gun
- Dry oasis foam
- Knife
- Waxed florist's tape
- Twig-edged wire frame
- Secateurs

Natural materials
- Preserved palm leaves
- Twigs
- Moss
- Plumosin (marigolds)
- Preserved protea

...and some tips!

- *If twig-edged wire frames are not available they are not absolutely necessary to hold the stems in place, as this is done by the oasis.*

A smooth base

1 The end of the drainpipe will be quite rough so it needs to be covered. This helps to keep the oasis in place and also prevents the stems from coming through. Stand the pipe on the cardboard and draw around it with the pen. Cut out the circle of card and glue it in place. Fill the pipe with oasis, cutting the pieces to size with a knife.

Strengthening the leaves

2 If the palm leaves are long, cut them into sections, making sure the cut ends are straight. The leaves will be too thick to push directly into the foam, so twig stems are attached. Open out the leaf and glue a twig along the centre at the bottom end. Add more glue and close the leaf tightly around the stick until the glue has set. For extra strength, bind over the glued section with waxed florist's tape, gently pulling the tape as you wind it round. *Remember the heat of your hands softens the wax on the tape and then it hardens again as it cools.*

Positioning the frame

3 Put a fine layer of moss over the oasis in the top of the pipe to cover it. Fit the twig-edged wire frame over the top of the pot, pushing it firmly down into place.

Outline shape

4 Begin the arrangement by building up the initial outline shape using the palm leaves. Start in the centre, pushing the twig stems of the leaves straight into the foam and work towards the sides, gradually placing them at an angle.

Adding colour

5 If necessary, trim down the flower stems and add these to the arrangement, frequently turning the container to ensure that a good balance of colour and texture is being achieved. Add the larger protea flowers last and finish the outer edge with a few shorter palm leaves.

Bunches of simple country grasses fill these pretty painted pots, but they could be filled with any type of arrangement – just use your imagination.

Whispering grass

What you need...

- Plain long tom terracotta pot
- Acrylic paint and brush
- Elastic band
- Decorative pen
- Dry oasis foam
- Knife
- Medium gauge florist's wire
- Scissors

Natural materials
- Setaria grass
- Moss

...and some tips!

- *Try painting stripes and checks on the pots or use a paint stamp to coordinate with your interior.*

The first coat

1 Make sure that the pot is clean and dry before you paint it. Apply an even coat of paint over the surface, allow it to dry and repeat the process. *The paint will be absorbed rapidly by the terracotta, but two coats should be sufficient to give an even coverage.*

Decorative touch

2 When the paint is completely dry, add a decoration around the top of the pot. This is done by writing the name of the grass used in the arrangement. Place an elastic band around the pot at the level you require the writing. Mark the pot with a few dots as a guide line. Write the grass name repeatedly around the pot, leaving a small gap between each word. Fill the pot with oasis foam, cutting it to size with a knife (see page 134).

Completing the arrangement

3 Separate the grass into small bunches of varying heights. Trim the stems and wire each bunch (see page 132). This will prevent the stems bending when pushed into the foam. Start by inserting the largest bunches in the centre of the oasis, then fill the remaining foam, placing the bunches close together to give a solid block of grass. Cover any visible foam around the edges with small pieces of moss. *While you are arranging the bunches of grass, remember to turn the pot frequently to check on the overall shape.*

Framed heart

What you need...

- Ruler
- Double sided frame
- Pen
- Cardboard
- Scissors
- Glue gun
- Fine gold wire

Natural materials
- Green moss
- Red rose petal

...and some tips!

- *When measuring the frame, allow a little extra space as the moss will add to the size of the heart.*

This moss heart can be made to fit any picture frame and its natural simplicity makes it an ideal decoration for any room.

Cutting out

1 Measure the window in the frame and use this size to calculate the size of the heart. Draw the heart shape on to the cardboard, remembering to allow for the moss when deciding on its size. Cut out the cardboard heart.

A moss covering

2 Spread hot glue on one side of the heart, allow to cool slightly, then press on a piece of moss. The piece of moss should cover the whole surface and overlap the sides. Once the glue is dry, trim off any excess moss to give a crisp edge to your heart. Repeat this process on the other side of the heart.

Finishing touches

3 Holding the heart in one hand and the reel of gold wire in the other, begin to wind the wire around the heart in a random pattern. Place the rose petal in the centre of the heart and continue winding the wire round several more times. Cut off the end of the wire and push it into the side of the heart, securing with a tiny spot of glue if necessary. Sandwich the heart between the two sides of the frame.

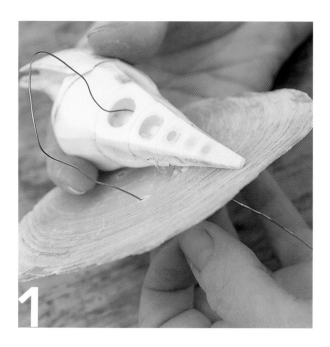

Starfish wreath

What you need...

- Glue gun and glue
- Florist's wire
- Scissors
- Cutters
- Drill
- Plastic eggs

Natural materials
- Grey twig wreath
- Oyster shell slices
- Starfish
- Pointed trimmed shells
- Carolina thistles
- Poppies

...and some tips!

- *Be careful when handling the Carolina thistles as they can be very prickly.*

Wonderful neutral colours and an abundance of interesting textures. A perfect wreath for the bathroom.

Oyster shells

1 Using the drill, with a small drill bit, make two holes in the centre of the oyster shell slices, approximately 1–2 cm (½–1 inch) apart. Now drill two holes at either side of the starfish. Pull a long piece of florist's wire through the centre of the pointed shells, then pull the wires down through the holes in the oyster shell, securing the two together. Thread a length of wire through each of the holes in the starfish, securing them tightly so that they can be tied onto the wreath.

Balancing effect

2 Trim the Carolina thistles and poppies, leaving a short stem of approximately 1–2 cm (½–1 inch). Lay the ingredients out on top of the wreath in their groupings and check that the overall effect is balanced.

Wiring and gluing

3 Begin attaching the large shells first, pulling their wires tightly around the wreath, securing them at the back. Glue the Carolina thistles and poppies next to the shells, pushing the stems down into the wreath. This makes them more secure. Finally, add the eggs, again using a generous amount of glue, pressing down firmly until the glue has cooled. Add a hanging loop of wire to the back of the wreath.

Natural tones

Natural tones of pale wood, shiny exotic seed pods, raffia and grasses, make this decorated box ideal for contemporary or rustic home interiors.

Creating a key

1 Use sandpaper to create a 'key' on the back of the seed pods as they have an extremely shiny surface which will not adhere well. Spread glue on to the surface of the pods and on to the appropriate areas of the wooden planter where they will be stuck.

If the seed pods you have chosen have a rougher texture, this will not be necessary. Instead, just use a standard glue gun.

Stuck fast

2 Leave for the recommended time before placing the pods on to the box, then hold down firmly so that the two glued surfaces bond together. Leave until completely set.

Arrange the pods in any pattern which looks good on the box; we have placed them close together, one above the other.

Bundling up

3 Fill the box with oasis foam, cutting it to size with a knife (see page 134). Take a small handful of wheat stems and cut down to make a short compact bundle. Wind wire around the middle to secure the stems and trim the ends level. Cover the wire with raffia, binding it round several times, then tie in a knot and cut off any excess. Spread glue along one edge of the box and on the back of the wheat bundle, leave for the recommended time, then press the bundle firmly on to the glued edge. Tie the grass stems tightly together. Using the sharp carving knife, cut straight through both ends of the bundle to leave the ends level. The stems should be cut long enough to be pushed into the oasis and still protrude above the rim of the box. Push a small handful at a time into the oasis until the box is full. Take a heavy book and tap the tops of the stems until they are even.

Tempting fruits

What you need...

- Pen
- Corrugated cardboard
- Scissors
- Glue gun
- Red and green spray paints
- Red and green thread

Natural materials
- Small twigs
- Red and green raffia
- Preserved leaves

...and some tips!

- *Don't make the apples any bigger than approximately 7 cm (3 inches), otherwise they look very clumsy.*

Red and green raffia apples make perfect decorations for Hallowe'en, or at any other time of year.

Taking shape

1 Draw an apple shape on to the corrugated cardboard, making sure the corrugations run from top to bottom. Cut it out using scissors. Cut a twig down to size, apply a little glue to one end and insert it into the top of the apple to form a stalk. Spray the apple with spray paint, allowing one side to dry before spraying the other.

Wrapping it up

2 Separate the strands of raffia and tie 13 or 14 lengths together to form one extremely long piece. Trim off the loose ends around the knots. Wind one end of the raffia around the apple and tie tightly, then continue to wind, changing direction gradually to eventually cover the cardboard.

It doesn't matter if little bits of cardboard are visible between strands of raffia as they are the same colour.

Adding a leaf

3 When the whole apple is covered, secure the end of the raffia with a small dot of glue at the base of the stalk. To ensure the raffia is held firmly in place, wind matching-coloured thread over it randomly, again securing the end with some glue at the stalk. Make a thread hanging loop and glue to the base of the stalk. Finally glue a leaf over the top to cover everything up.

20–30 minutes

Bright yellow lemons nestle amongst glossy dark green leaves in a Victorian metal urn – the perfect design for a formal setting.

Victorian lemon

What you need...

- Secateurs
- Artificial lemons
- Glue gun
- Metal urn
- Dry oasis foam
- Knife
- Dry oasis foam ball
- Mossing pins

Natural materials
- Preserved green salal leaves
- Twig
- Woodland moss

...and some tips!

- *Remember, it takes a lot more foliage than you think to cover the foam ball, so don't choose one that is too big.*

Preparing the materials

1 Trim down the stems of the leaves to the correct length at a suitable joint. Do the same with the lemons, or if they are not wired, attach a stem with hot glue. Trim the twig to be used as the trunk, making it pointed at either end so it is much easier to push into the oasis. Fill the metal urn with oasis foam, cutting it to shape with a knife (see page 134). Place the sharpened branch into the centre of the oasis and push it down until it hits the bottom of the urn. Now fix the oasis ball on top, inserting the trunk to a depth of at least half the ball's height.

Adding foliage

2 Start to build up a framework of leaves, inserting the stems at least 2 cm (1 inch) into the foam so that they are firmly fixed. Support the ball as you push in the stems, so that it doesn't become loose. *Concentrate on just one section of the ball at a time and complete this before you move onto the next.*

Filling gaps

3 As you add more leaves to each section, push small amounts of moss between the stems, holding it in place with mossing pins. This covers any visible oasis and also gives a good background to the glossy leaves. Once the whole ball is covered in leaves, add the trimmed stems of lemons. Begin at the top of the tree and make sure that the lemons are put in randomly, turning the tree frequently to check their spacing. Finally, cover the oasis in the urn with a thick blanket of moss.

Herbal harvest

What you need...

- Fine string
- Chicken wire square
- Masking tape
- Scissors
- Glue gun

Natural materials
- Wheat
- Dried orange slice (see page 134)
- Preserved rosemary
- Dried gold achillea
- 2 bay leaves

...and some tips!

- *Try experimenting with different shapes and sizes for the frame such as an oval or heart shape.*

A chicken wire frame, decorated with a herb and citrus bouquet and surrounded with harvest wheat. The perfect decoration for a kitchen window.

Basic framework

1 Tie a small hanging loop of string to one edge of the chicken wire. Cover all four edges of the wire square with masking tape on both sides, to act as a base for the wheat and also to cover the sharp edges of the wire. Cut the wheat heads off the stems, trim eight stems to length and glue two stems to each of the frame sides.

Making a border

2 Starting on the outside edge of the frame, glue the wheat heads in a row all facing the same direction, with each head covering the stem of the previous one. Complete one square, then repeat twice, finishing with three rows forming a broad border. *Carefully cut the wheat heads to size if necessary, to fit the frame.*

Decorative finish

3 Cut the orange slice in half. Trim the rosemary and achillea into small sprigs and tie together with string to form a little bouquet. Glue two bay leaves in a 'V'-shape onto the centre of the wire frame. Take a piece of the orange and glue it next to the base of the leaves, with the rosemary bouquet on top. Finally, cover the string on the bouquet by gluing the second piece of orange on top.

Soft and romantic, a subtle palette of blues and purples is captured in this simple wreath.

Hydrangea wreath

What you need...

- Paper string
- 2 double-ended tassels
- Glue gun

Natural materials
- Dried hydrangea heads
- Willow twig wreath

...and some tips!

- *Hydrangeas can fade quite quickly, but the wreath can be rejuvenated by applying spray paint. It will look incredible sprayed with a fresh lime green or gold.*

- *For a stunning effect, display the hydrangea wreath against a crisp white background.*

Tying the knot

1 Sort through the hydrangea heads and separate the large pieces into smaller sprigs. Fold the paper string in half and tie a knot approximately 8 cm (3 inches) from the fold. This will be the hanging loop.

Attaching the tassels

2 Lay the knotted string on a work surface and place the wreath over it. Lay the two double-ended tassels across the top of the wreath, at right angles to the hanging loop. Bring the two loose ends of the string through the centre of the wreath and up over the tassels. Pass them through the two pieces of string below the knot in the hanging loop then pull tightly and bind the ropes around the wreath, again securing them with a simple knot at the back under the hanging loop.

Building up the display

3 When the loop is held firmly in position, turn the wreath over and lay it down flat. Take small pieces of hydrangea and glue them in place between the willow twigs to cover the wreath. This will give a wonderful mass of colours and textures. *Arrange the flowers close together, but without crushing them as they are very delicate. It is this wreath's simplicity that is its strength.*

Shaker simplicity

What you need...

- Dry oasis foam
- Knife
- Heart-shaped cookie cutter
- Glue gun
- Green thread
- Skewer
- Scissors
- Garden twine
- Medium gauge florist's wire
- Checked ribbon

Natural materials
- Moss
- Dried red roses

...and some tips!

- *Steam the rose heads to revitalize their shape if necessary, before gluing them to the hearts (see page 132).*

This sweet and simple heart and rose swag was inspired by Shaker philosophy.

Taking shape

1 Cut three slices of foam then cut a heart out of each using the cookie cutter. Spread hot glue on to one side of each heart at a time. Stick on small pieces of moss until the whole surface is covered. Wind the dark green thread around the hearts randomly to give added security and a more defined shape. Gently push the skewer through the centre of each heart from top to bottom. (Push the skewer through slowly and carefully to avoid splitting the hearts).

Loop the loop

2 Cut some garden twine to the desired length of the swag, adding a little extra for a hanging loop. Attach the end of the twine to the end of a

length of wire. Double the wire over and twist the ends together. The finished length of wire must be long enough to go through the hole in each heart, plus extra to spare. Carefully push the wire through one of the hearts, then pull the twine through.

Stringing up

3 Tie a knot in the twine to stop the heart sliding down. A spot of glue on the knot will give added security. Repeat, adding the second and third hearts, finishing off with a knot at the tip of the final heart. Trim off any excess twine.

Winding twine

4 Cut the rose heads off the stems and gather the stems into three bundles. Wind twine around the bundles and secure with a knot. Trim the bundles to equal sizes and attach to the swag by gluing to the twine. Glue the rose heads gently but firmly to the hearts. Tie the top of the twine into a hanging loop, make a simple ribbon bow and glue it over the knot.

The bundles of stems will look most attractive if they still have the leaves attached to them.

Stunning pink peonies mingle with creamy white achillea, dusky pink larkspur and nigella in a pretty hand-tied bouquet, perfect for a sumptuous gift.

Bountiful bouquet

What you need...

- Medium gauge florist's wire
- Green crêpe tape
- Scissors
- Ribbon

Natural materials
- Silica-dried peonies
- Achillea ptarmica
- Dusky pink larkspur
- *Nigella orientalis*
- *Lepidium*

...and some tips!

- *Take care when levelling the stems. The bouquet should be level enough to stand unaided on a flat surface.*

Central core

1 Start by making a small mixed bunch of all the ingredients, putting a peony in the middle. Place the bunch in one hand and add about three stems of each flower and grass (except the peonies which should be added individually) at a time to build up the bunch. Once you have used a third of the material, wrap a piece of wire around the bunch to hold the stems in place. Cover the wire with crêpe tape.

As you continue to build up the bouquet, add the stems at a slight angle, turning the bouquet as you work. As you angle the stems more, you will begin to create a soft dome of flowers.

All tied up

2 When you are happy with the arrangement, tie a wire around the stems several times before securing it. Cover the wire with crêpe tape. Trim off the bottoms of the stems to make the base level. If it is slightly unsteady, hold it in both hands and tap it gently on the work surface to even the base without altering the shape of the bouquet. Add a ribbon to conceal the crêpe tape around the centre.

A stunning Christmas wreath of twigs and oak leaves, brought to life by glistening gold cobs of dried corn.

Festive wreath

What you need...

- Secateurs
- Glue gun
- Gold spray paint
- Medium gauge florist's wire

Natural materials
- Preserved and dyed oak
- Open weave twig wreath
- Dried corn cobs with husks

...and some tips!

- *Always make sure that the room is well ventilated when using spray paint and that all surfaces are well protected. Try and do all spraying outside if possible.*

- *It is very important to use a wreath which has a wide, open weave, otherwise it will be difficult to glue the stems in place.*

Building up the wreath

1 Separate the oak branches into small sprigs. Place a generous amount of glue on the end of an oak sprig and insert it into the weave of the wreath. Hold it in place until the glue is dry and it is securely held in place. Add the rest of the oak sprigs in the same way until the top of the wreath is covered, gluing them randomly and at varying angles. This gives the design a wonderfully informal and textured appeal. Gently peel back the husks on the corn cobs to give them the appearance of petals. Spray the cobs with gold paint, coating one side at a time, until they are all evenly covered.

Golden highlights

2 Divide the corn cobs into pairs and arrange on the wreath, checking that the overall appearance is balanced. Using a generous amount of glue on the back of each cob, stick them in position, gluing directly to the wreath and not to the oak leaves, otherwise they will fall off when the wreath is hung. To hang your finished wreath, attach a wire through the open twigs to make a loop.

over 30 minutes

Silver sparkler

What you need...

- Mixing bowl and spoon
- Multi-purpose plaster
- Square metal pot
- Fine gravel
- Secateurs
- Scissors
- Thick plain paper
- Dry oasis cone
- Glue gun
- Silver spray paint
- Medium gauge florist's wire
- Metal icing nozzle

Natural materials
- Small stick
- Grey moss or lichen
- Preserved eucalyptus

...and some tips!

- *If you can't find a metal icing nozzle, a simple cone of card, sprayed silver is a suitable substitute.*

This elegant tree, with its pendulous leaves, contrasts brilliantly with the clear, sharp lines of the sparkly silver top.

A firm base

1 Using the bowl and spoon, mix up the plaster according to the manufacturer's instructions. Check that the inside of the metal pot is free from grease and dust. Add several handfuls of gravel to the plaster to give extra bulk and cut down on drying time. Trim the stick to be used for the trunk, making it pointed at one end. Remove any loose bark or dirt from the blunt end. Fill the pot with the plaster, then push the base of the trunk into the middle of the pot. Leave to set hard.

Preparing the tree

2 Cut out a wedge of paper large enough to cover the foam cone. Glue the paper over the cone and spray silver. Glue a band of moss or lichen to the bottom edge of the cone. Trim the eucalyptus down to shorter lengths, approximately half the length of the cone. Cut about 30 short lengths of wire and bend to form staples. Lay a piece of eucalyptus on the cone, stem up, with the leaves overlapping the base. Secure it in place using one or two staples pushed into the oasis. Add glue if necessary. Add more pieces of eucalyptus in the same way around the cone to make the first layer.

Tip top

3 Add the rest of the eucalyptus in the same way moving higher up the cone with each layer. Trim off the stems at the top of the cone and bind with wire to give a neat tight finish. Glue a band of moss around the bottom of the piping nozzle. Apply a generous amount of glue to the top of the cone and glue the nozzle in place. Turn the tree upside down and mark the centre point on the base. Insert the pointed trunk into the tree, push the tree firmly down over the mark. Finish off the base with enough moss to cover any exposed plaster.

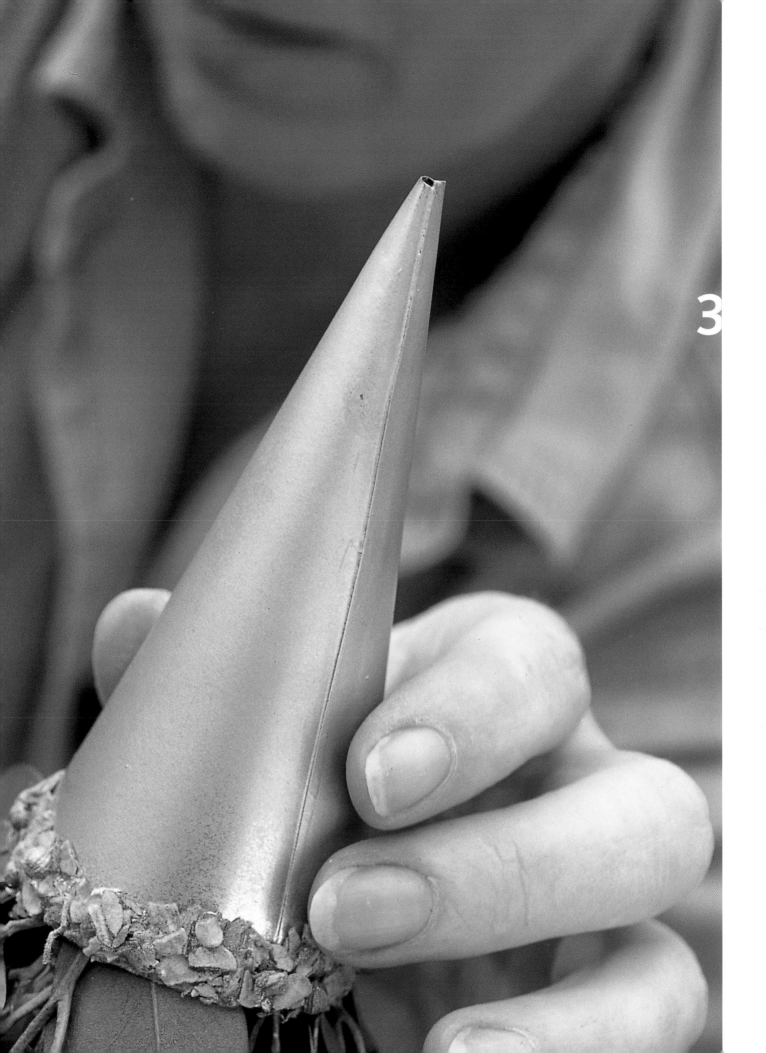

Rustic table

What you need...

- Lemon gloss paint
- Paint brush
- Ruler
- Pencil
- Chicken wire
- Wire cutters
- Thick gloves (optional)
- Staple gun

Natural materials
- Wooden table
- 4 pieces of wooden batten (same length as the table top)
- Moss
- Dried sunflowers (see page 134)

...and some tips!

- *Although good for summer entertaining, do not leave the table out in bright sunlight for too long as the moss will start to fade quite quickly.*

Serve the perfect summer lunch from this pretty, rustic lemon table with its moss and golden sunflower border.

Measuring up

1 Paint the table lemon, preparing the wood first if necessary and leave to dry. Measure and mark a 15 cm (6 inch) border around the outer edge of the table top. Roll out the chicken wire and cut four strips, 30 cm (12 inches) deep. Cut two strips the same length as the shortest sides of the table. Then two pieces which are 20 cm (8 inches) longer than the side of the table.

You may want to wear protective gloves while cutting the wire.

3

Fixing the wire

2 Starting with the two shorter ends of the table, lay a strip of wire, parallel with the table edge, about 2.5 cm (1 inch) inside the marked line with the rest of the strip towards the centre of the table. Using the staple gun, fix the wire securely along the guideline. Then repeat this with the other end of the table.

Bending over

3 Place the wooden batten on top of the secured wire with its edge along the marked line and the rest of the batten towards the outside of the table. Hold it firmly in place with one hand and fold the wire over the batten towards the table edge.

4

A thick layer

4 Sort through the moss and shake off any excess earth. Place a layer of moss under the wire, forming a solid block. This should completely cover the painted surface under the wire. *If you have small pieces of moss and they are falling off the sides, a small amount of glue will hold them securely in place.*

Pulling tight

5 Pull the wire tightly over the moss and secure it under the table edges using the staple gun. Attach the long strips of wire to the table in the same way, leaving an equal overlap of wire at either end. Bend the wire back over the batten and then add the moss as before.

Adding structure

6 Place four sunflower heads together in each corner, in a square pattern. Secure the wire underneath the table with staples to give a neat edge. *Depending on the shape of the table, you may have to trim off some of the wire around the legs to achieve a neat finish.*

6

Coffee bean tree

What you need...

- Newspaper
- Border adhesive
- Brush
- Dry oasis foam ball
- Bowl of water
- Dry oasis foam cone
- Brown emulsion paint
- Knife
- Glue gun
- Dry oasis foam block

Natural materials
- Butter beans
- Soya beans
- Coffee beans
- Cinnamon sticks
- Bamboo cane
- Terracotta flowerpot

...and some tips!

- *If you find it difficult to glue your first row of beans in a straight line, attach an elastic band around the centre of the ball and use it as a guide.*

- *This tree is well suited to a window ledge as it won't fade as fast as dried flowers or foliage.*

Dark aromatic coffee beans mingle with cinnamon and pulses in a spicily scented, sculptural display.

All wrapped up

1 Tear the newspaper into small strips.
Apply border adhesive to the surface
of the oasis ball. Dip a paper strip in
water and then lay on to the ball
smoothing out any folds with your
fingertips. Cover the ball completely
and repeat with the oasis cone. Leave
to dry.

Applying paint

2 Paint both shapes, taking care to cover all the newsprint, and allow to dry. Apply two coats if necessary. Spread out the beans on a work surface and divide into different piles according to type and size.

Preparing the materials

3 Cut the cinnamon sticks into short, equal lengths. These will be used to decorate the cone and cover the trunk. *A sharp knife should be used for this as they can be very brittle. Remove any loose layers and set aside to decorate the base.*

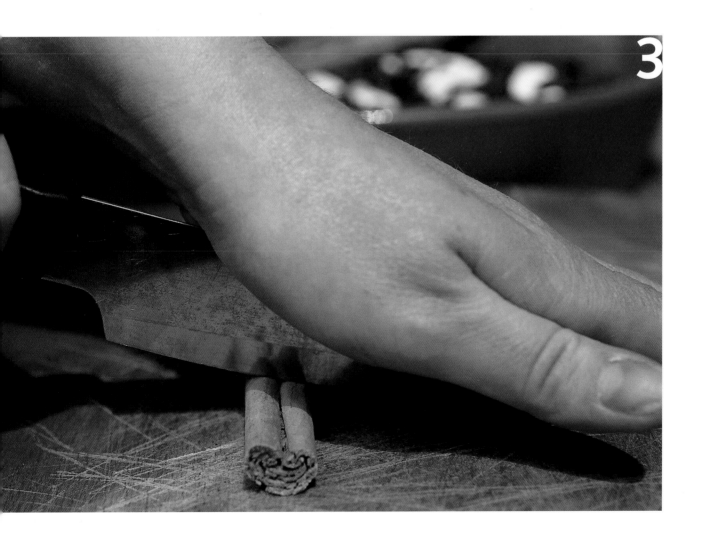

Creating a pattern

4 Glue a row of butter beans around the centre of the oasis ball. Check that the beans are clean and the skins are not split, otherwise they will not stick. Add a row of soya beans and a row of coffee beans. When you come to the last few in a row, remember to lay them on before gluing to check that they are going to fit. Make a small hole in the top of the ball, checking that it is central. Hold the ball in one hand and push the cane through the ball, keeping it as straight as possible.

It must be pushed through far enough to allow the cone to be attached securely on top and have a small section of trunk showing.

Decorating the cone

5 Decorate the cone in the same way, starting at the bottom edge and working upwards to the tip. Add a row of cinnamon stick pieces between the rows of beans. The underside of the cone does not have to be covered with beans. *When using the coffee beans, glue them on in different ways to show both sides. This adds more texture to the finished design.*

Making a trunk

6 Take several of the cinnamon stick pieces and split them in half lengthways using the knife. Glue these over the cane to cover a short section either side of the ball. These sections will form the trunk of the tree. Do not cover the ends of the cane as these will not be seen once the tree is complete. Add the remaining beans to complete the decoration of the ball.

Planting the tree

7 Push one end of the cane into the centre of the cone base. Insert it up to the level of the cinnamon, keeping it as straight as possible. Fill the terracotta pot with foam, cutting it to fit with a knife, and 'plant' your tree in the centre. Use the remaining cinnamon pieces to cover the foam around the base of the tree.

Chilli heart

What you need...

- Pen
- Corrugated cardboard
- Craft knife
- Glue gun
- Masking tape (optional)
- Red spray paint
- Medium gauge florist's wire
- Clear spray varnish

Natural materials
- Red raffia
- Dried red chillies

...and some tips!

- *Avoid hanging the heart near the oven or sink where there may be excess heat or moisture. This may affect the appearance of the chillies.*

- *Don't make the cardboard heart too large or you will need a huge number of chillies to cover it.*

- *Warning: don't touch your eyes or lips when working with chillies; wash your hands immediately on completion.*

Hot! Hot! Hot! A simple heart spiced up with red hot chilli peppers. Perfect for the kitchen.

Taking shape

1 Draw a heart shape on the cardboard and cut it out with a craft knife. Using the first shape as a template, draw around it and cut out a second heart. Glue the two hearts together. Although not absolutely essential, it is advisable to bind the hearts with masking tape. This makes for a much more robust frame. Before you bind all the way round, tie a length of raffia into a hanging loop and glue it into place between the hearts at the top.

Adding colour

2 Finish binding the tops of the hearts together with the masking tape. Spray the hearts with red spray paint on both sides. Apply two coats if necessary for an even coverage.

Work in a well-ventilated room or, even better, outside. Remember to protect all work surfaces.

Side one

3 Divide the chillies into piles of straight and curved ones. Wire together the straight chillies into groups of three (see page 132) and cut off the wire ends. Starting in the centre at the top of the heart, glue a bunch of chillies on the heart, with the tips pointing towards the 'V' of the heart. Add a bunch on either side facing the same direction, but with the tips pointing outwards over the side of the heart. Continue to add rows in this way, using the tips of the chillies to cover the wired ends of the previous row. When the first half is complete, use the individual curved chillies to fill in the gaps and give the heart added texture.

Completing the heart

4 Start the second half of the heart back at the top. The bunches of chillies must now be glued on in the opposite direction. Finish the second side in the same way as the first. Spray the heart with clear varnish to give a rich glossy finish and help to preserve the chillies.

A classic obelisk decorated with woodland moss, seeds and leaves, to give it a modern twist.

Old world charm

What you need...

- Ruler
- Pencil
- Corrugated cardboard
- Scissors
- Masking tape
- Border adhesive
- Dark green thread
- Glue gun
- Reel wire

Natural materials
- Moss
- Butterfly seed pods
- Natural cord
- Sprigs of preserved leaves
- 5 small wooden balls

...and some tips!

- *If you are short of time, use larger leaves rather than making small wired bundles, and spray the card with green paint rather than mossing it.*

Cardboard cut outs

1 Cut four identical tall triangles and one square out of the corrugated cardboard. Tape the triangles together to form an obelisk, securing the 90° joints with masking tape. Attach the square base in the same way.

Chopping the moss

2 Sort through the moss, picking out any pieces of twig. Take a handful of moss at a time and cut it into small pieces using scissors. This will give a much more even finish than gluing on larger pieces.

An even covering

3 Spread the border adhesive on one side of the obelisk. Sprinkle the finely chopped moss generously over the glue. Press down firmly to ensure it adheres properly. Repeat on all sides of the obelisk and leave to dry.

Winding up

4 Choose the best seed pods to decorate the sides. These must graduate in size: smaller ones for the top of the obelisk and larger ones for the base. Tie the green thread to the top of the obelisk and wind it around four times, with each ring an equal distance apart, finishing at a corner of the base. Glue the end of the thread to secure it. Check that all four sides look even before proceeding. Stick the seed pods onto the obelisk, starting with the smallest at the top. Glue each in the

centre of a side, over the thread guideline. Glue the cord to the top of the obelisk and wrap it around, following the thread and passing over the seed pods. Pull the cord firmly and glue it in place at the bottom.

A leafy spiral

5 Arrange the leaf sprigs into small bunches, binding the stems with wire to secure them tightly. Use the bunches to form a spiral of leaves, winding them around the obelisk between the rings of cord. Start by gluing the first bunch over the end of the cord at the top, with the stems pointing down. Add each bunch of leaf sprigs in turn, using the leaves to cover the stems of the previous bunch, and following the line of the cord down the obelisk. Cover the wire on the last bunch by gluing two or three individual leaves on top.

Adding the feet

6 Fix a wooden ball to each of the 4 corners of the base of your obelisk, using a generous amount of glue. Add the last ball to the top of the obelisk to complete your design.

A touch of opulence: deepest green glossy magnolia leaves create a stunning frame for this grand wall mirror.

Magnolia mirror

What you need...

- Rectangular mirror
- Plywood rectangle
- Pencil
- Dark green gloss paint
- Paint brush
- Metal hanging hook
- Contact adhesive
- Pile of heavy books
- Medium gauge florist's wire
- Wire cutters

Natural materials
- Preserved and dyed magnolia leaves

...and some tips!

- *Preserved dyed leaves may colour your hands so wash them frequently to avoid staining.*

First impressions

1 Lay the mirror in the centre of the plywood and mark around the outline. Remove the mirror. Paint the marked border with the dark green gloss paint, preparing the wood first, if necessary. When dry, attach the hanging hook to the back of the panel. Spread contact adhesive to the back of the mirror and the unpainted centre of the board. When the adhesive is tacky, lay the mirror onto the board. Check that the alignment is correct then weigh down with heavy books and leave until dry. Spread the leaves out and pick out the four largest for the corners. Divide the others into piles of three different sizes. Take a leaf of each size and wire together (see page 132) with the largest leaf in the centre and glossy sides upwards. Half of the bundles should be wired with the three leaves flat and the other half with the three leaves at different angles. Glue a large leaf to each corner of the frame, each pointing outwards with the glossy side up. Then start to build up the first layer of leaves.

Making the frame

2 Arrange the flat bunches on the frame with their tips overhanging the sides, disguising its hard, straight edge. Work on one side at a time, checking that the bunches are evenly spaced and the outline is balanced. Glue them in place and repeat until your first layer is complete.

Layering leaves

3 The second, inside layer of leaves can now be built up. This layer should cover the stems of the first layer around the edge of the mirror. Lay down the bundles at an angle to the other leaves, almost parallel to the mirror edge, working around the frame in one direction. Use each bunch of leaves to cover the stems of the last bunch. Check the overall shape of the design and glue in place when you are satisfied with it. This time you only have to glue the largest central leaf in the bunch to the frame. The other two leaves can be left unattached giving more depth and texture to the finished mirror.

Techniques

Wiring

It is often necessary to wire individual flower stems to either make them stronger, and thus easier to work with, or to make them longer, allowing them to be inserted into oasis foam. Wiring techniques are also used to join several stems into a bunch when the display requires them to be arranged in this way. Wiring is easily done and only requires practice to achieve a secure, neat finish. Bend the wire into a 'U'-shape approximately two-thirds along its length. This produces one end longer than the other. Place the bent wire behind the stem with the wires running parallel to it and the bend at the top. Hold the stem and the short end of the wire firmly together and wrap the long end neatly around them. Bind this wire around several times, working down towards the end of the stem. When this is completed, the two ends should be almost equal in length.

Adding a new stem

Often dried flowers, such as roses, are sold without stems at all, making them difficult to wire. The easiest solution is to glue the flower head onto the top of a wheat stem. These stems are quite sturdy and also hollow, which makes it easy to attach the flower head.

Steaming roses

When buying bunches of dried roses, you often find that the flower heads are squashed and misshapen. This can be fixed by holding the rose head downwards over the spout of a boiling kettle. The steam moistens the petals and they are then easily pulled back into shape. This must be done gently as the rose petals are very delicate. Only hold the rose over the steam for a few seconds until the petals start to waiver.

Drying oranges

The best results are achieved by allowing the oranges to dry slowly. If you want to dry whole oranges, choose small fruits. Cut slits in the sides or pierce the top and bottom. This is essential to allow the juices to drain away. Alternatively, cut the orange into slices. Place the fruits on a wire cooling tray and place in a very cool oven to dry. This takes quite a long time, depending on the thickness of the fruit. Do not be tempted to turn the oven up as they will turn a horrible dark brown colour. Other fruits which work well are pomegranates and rose hips.

Filling containers with foam

Dry oasis foam is one of the most useful materials used in dried flower arrangements. It is quick and easy to use, but care needs to be taken when cutting, as particles of oasis can irritate the eyes. When filling a container with foam, it is most important that it is a snug fit and does not spring out. This is easily done with smaller containers by placing the container on top of the foam and marking around it. Cut out the shape and shave off wedges of foam if the container has sloping sides. When using containers much larger than the oasis blocks, you may need to bind the blocks together using florist's tape before fitting. This will ensure that one piece does not spring out or lay at a different level from the rest. The golden rule is to make sure that the oasis is securely fixed before you start a design.

Drying flowers

Air drying This is by far the easiest method of drying flowers. In most cases flowers can be allowed to dry out slowly, by hanging them upside down in a cool, airy place. If they dry out too quickly, they may become very brittle and difficult to work with. Should you decide to buy fresh flowers for drying, separate out the stems and make them into smaller bunches before drying. Have fun and experiment with more unusual varieties. Many flowers dry well but are not sold commercially because they are too difficult to transport.

Water drying This is also a very simple method, but not often used. This works particularly well for flowers such as hydrangeas. Sit the stems in a glass or jar containing 5 cm (2 inches) of water and leave in a cool, dry place. Allow the water to evaporate: by the time the container is dry, so are the flowers.

Microwave This is a good drying method for leaves and pot pourri ingredients, with instant results. Place a few sheets of kitchen paper in the microwave as a base. Sprinkle petals or herbs on top and cook on a medium to full heat for 1–2 minutes. The time depends on the quantity and size of the materials being dried. Test them to see if they feel dry, then remove from the microwave and allow to cool. Try experimenting with

different ingredients. Ovens vary so this process is very much trial and error.

Silica gel crystals This is a very successful method for retaining the shape and colour of flowers, but the crystals are expensive and not terribly easy to find. Excellent results can be achieved, especially with zinnias and roses. The flowers are immersed in layers of crystals which draw the moisture from them. The crystals can be reused.

Glycerine This method is mainly used for foliage – beech and oak leaves work well. Always choose materials which are in perfect condition, otherwise the results will be disappointing. Trim the ends of the stems and then hammer them so that they split. Stand them in a 50/50 solution of glycerine and hot water that is approximately 15 cm (6 inches) deep. Remove the stems from the solution when they have stopped taking up the liquid.

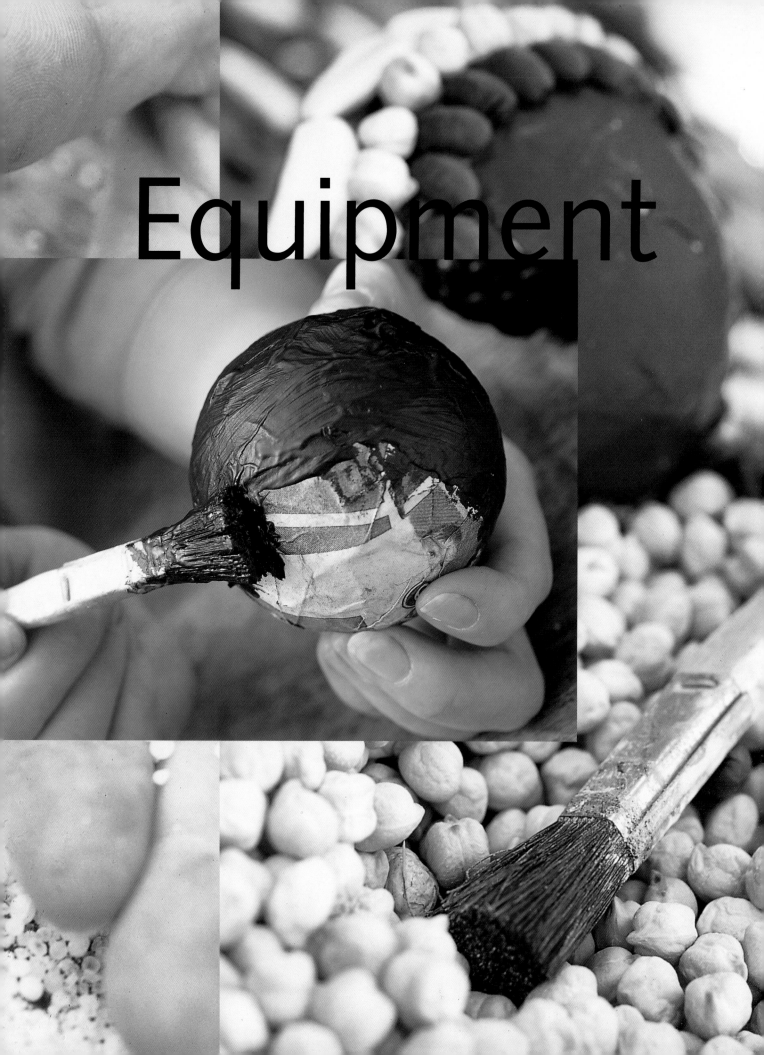

Equipment

To create displays like the ones in this book, it is essential to have a few basic tools. This really does make a difference to both the finished product and the enjoyment of producing a design.

Glue gun

This is the main weapon in your florist's armoury. It is indispensable in so many designs due to the speed at which the glue melts. For those who are new to dried flowers, it practically eliminates the need for wiring materials and produces a more professional end product. The best buy is a Low Melt Gun which is designed to melt the glue at a lower temperature– so no more burnt fingers!

Dry oasis foam

A foam which is specifically designed for use with dried materials. It comes in two different colours: grey which is the traditional foam and now green which is manufactured by a more environmentally-friendly method. There are a variety of shapes available: cones, spheres and the most widely used, the standard block.

Florist's wires

These are designed for use by professional florists but after a little practice, can be used just as effectively by you! They are either pre-cut to the most popular lengths (also called stub wires) but also come in reels. Always choose the appropriate gauge of wire; the thicker and heavier the stems you are wiring, the thicker the wire should be. It is available in many colours such as grey, green, gold, red and silver.

Scissors

You don't have to have special florist's scissors but whatever you choose, make sure that they are strong, sharp and comfortable to work with. Don't attempt to cut wire with them: they will blunt quickly so use wire cutters instead. A smaller, sharper pair of scissors is also useful for cutting ribbons, paper, raffia, or indeed anything which requires a smooth clean cut edge.

Mossing pins

These simple wire staples can be bought ready-made, or are easy to make at home. Simply bend short lengths of wire into a 'U'-shape. They are good for attaching a variety of materials, especially moss, to a foam base.

Multi-purpose plaster

This is used to provide a secure base for the trunks in tree designs. It is easy to prepare, but takes quite a while to set, so does not give instant results like oasis.

Florist's clear spray sealant

Specially developed for use with dried materials, it acts like a light varnish. This is helpful when using materials which are delicate and it can also preserve the colour for slightly longer. You can use hairspray as an alternative, but use it sparingly.

Crêpe tape

The best tape to use if you need to cover wired stems or wires. It is stretchy and gives a very neat and professional finish. Available in white, green and brown.

Florist's spray paints

These paints have been specially developed for use with fresh and also dried materials without altering their texture. Wonderful for colour coordinating and great for giving faded arrangements a new lease of life, as they come in a wide choice of colours.

Craft knife

With its small sharp blade, it is a must for cutting out card shapes and also for sharpening twig ends to a point.

Large knife

Indispensable for cutting dry oasis foam, with a large flat blade and sturdy handle.

Containers

Traditionally, the most widely used container for dried arrangements has been the basket. Basketware today is available in a huge variety of textures, colours, shapes and sizes and by its very nature, works superbly with dried materials. If you decide to use a basket for a design, check to see if it needs to be lined before filling it with oasis; it is a pity to spoil an arrangement with pieces of foam showing through the weave. As most baskets are very light, remember to add weight to the base before starting a design. Also quickly check the underside of the basket for sharp edges which may scratch polished surfaces.

Index

Suppliers and Acknowledgements

Suppliers

There are a great many outlets today for dried flowers, supplies and containers, from farm shops to DIY superstores. Here are a few which I can recommend.

Acorn and Angels
33 The Boulevard
Antiques Village
Metro Centre
Gateshead
NE11 9YN

0191 4603262

Flowers, wreaths and containers, which are influenced by Shaker style.

Baileys Home and Garden
The Engine Shed
Ashburton Ind. Estate
Ross-on-Wye
Herefordshire

01989 563015

Interesting collection of containers, many one-off pieces as well as classical reproductions.

Chelsea Gardener
126 Sydney Street
Kings Road
London
SW3

0171 3525656

Great selection of terracotta and other containers.

Gail Armytage
51 High Street
Cowbridge
South Glamorgan
Wales
CF7 7AE

01446 772379

Flowers, ribbons, baskets, pots and everything else you may need. Mail order available.

Inscape
Great Western Road
Glasgow
Scotland
G4 0LF

0141 4001010

Dried and preserved flowers and foliage, basketware and metalware.

Mary Clark English Dried Flowers
High Risby,
Scunthorpe
South Humberside
DN15 0BU

01724 732151

Good quality English grown flowers. Mail order available.

Norpar Dried Flowers
Navestock Hall
Shonks Mill Road
Navestock
Essex
RM4 1HA

01277 374968

Wide selection of dried and preserved flowers, foliage and fruits, baskets and wreaths.

Potting Shed
13 London Road
Alderly Edge
Cheshire
SK9 7JT

01625 585819

Fantastic selection of pots, vases and many other interesting containers.

Roccoco
6 Greenwich Market
London
SE10 9HZ

0181 2933191

Flowers, baskets and many types of vases.

Style Workshop
39 High Street
Tunbridge Wells
Kent
TN1 1XL

01892 529636

A wonderful selection of unusual containers and flowers collected from all over Europe.

Terrace and Garden
Orchard House
Patmore End
Ugley, Bishops Sorford
CM22 6JA

01799 543289

A great variety of home and garden lifestyle products.

Acknowledgements

Special thanks to the team at Hamlyn; Polly, Mark and Cara and our photographer Linda with her willing assistant Maria. They all worked under very damp conditions but always with a smile.

To Martin and Tiryns who allowed me the luxury of writing this book in my garden under sunny blue skies.